SIMPLIFIED GUIDE TO JAZZ IMPROVISATION
Linear and Non-Linear

By Terry Janow

Published by

WORD PRODUCTIONS

PO Box 11184, Albuquerque, NM 87192

Simplified Guide to Jazz Improvisation
By Terry Janow

Copyright ©2020
By Terry Janow

ISBN: 978-1-7356273-1-1

Contact Terry Janow by visiting the Website:
https://www.janow4music.com

Published by:

WORD PRODUCTIONS LLC
PO Box 11184, Albuq., NM 87192
www.wordproductions.org

WORD PRODUCTIONS

Table of Contents

SIMPLIFIED GUIDE TO JAZZ IMPROVISATION
Linear and Non-Linear
By Terry Janow

Part I
Tonality and Scale Structure

1 . The key signature of a composition gives us far more information than just how many sharps or flats we have to remember as we play. The key signature also gives us a clue to the <u>tonality</u> of the composition. For example, if there was one sharp written as a key signature we would know that the song is in the tonality of either G major or E minor. The composer decided on the key of one sharp probably because the majority of the notes that comprise the composition are diatonic (belong) to the key of G.

2. The "Real Book" a popular compilation of leads sheets (melody & chords) has the song "Autumn Leaves" by Joseph Kosma with words by Johnny Mercer written with one Sharp (F#) as the key signature. However, the song ends on an E minor chord and consequently, "Autumn Leaves" is considered to be in the key of E minor. There are only three measures in the entire composition that contain notes that are chromatic (do not belong) to the key of G major. These notes happen to be C# and D# in the sixth measure, D# in measure sixteen, and A# in measure twenty four. However C# and D# are both diatonic to E melodic minor, and A# is diatonic to an E blues scale. The blues scale is a very widely used scale when in a minor key. We must conclude therefore, that a solo could be played using the key of G major, and any form of E minor as well as an E blues scale.

3. The major scale is the foundation for music of the "Western Civilization" All minor scales, modes, eight note diminished, eight note dominant, blues, lydian dominant, and many other commonly used scales are derived by altering or modifying a major scale. It is therefore, a good idea to understand the structure of a major scale

so you can understand how to recognize and manipulate it. The following diagram illustrates the C major scale on a keyboard. The notes of the C major scale occur on the white keys only. Notice that the pattern of intervals (distances) between each note in the C major scale is <u>whole-whole-half-(whole)-whole-whole-half</u>. All major scales are based on this pattern. If you play this pattern of intervals from any note you will create the sound of a major scale.

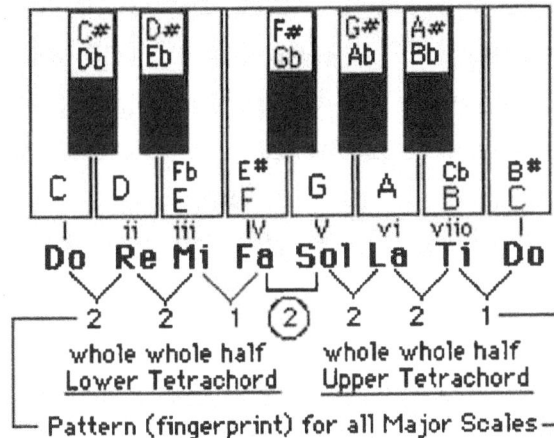

4. It is very important that you notice there are only two half steps. All other intervals are a whole step. Therefore, the half steps and where they are placed is the key to establishing tonality.

5. If you ever saw "The Sound of Music" with Julie Andrews you have heard people use the syllables Do-Re-Mi-Fa-Sol-La-Ti-Do. This is known as solfege (sol-fa in France) or solfeggio (sol-fa in Italy). Solfege is a universal major scale system that eliminates the need for key signatures. Do is always the first note of the major scale, Re is always the second note, Mi the third, Fa the fourth, Sol the fifth, La the sixth and finally Ti the seventh note of the major scale. The following diagram illustrates the active and resting quality of this pattern of intervals in the key of C major.

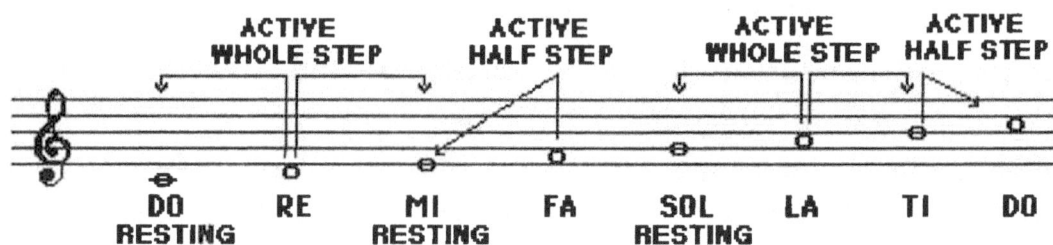

ACTIVE WHOLE STEP   **ACTIVE HALF STEP**   **ACTIVE WHOLE STEP**   **ACTIVE HALF STEP**

DO RESTING   RE   MI RESTING   FA   SOL RESTING   LA   TI   DO

6.   The previous diagram shows us that the active half step Fa (F), the fourth note of the major scale, and active half step Ti (B), the seventh note of the major scale move to the closest notes (resting tones) by half step.   The note Fa (F) moves downward to Mi (E) by halfstep, and the note Ti (B) moves upward to Do (Ti) by half step. This half step motion of Fa and Ti towards Do and Mi is much like gravity.   Everything in the universe is in motion towards a resting point.   In music, the half step motion of Fa and Ti establishes tonality.

7.   The following diagram illustrates what a dominant chord is and why it is considered dominant.   Every other letter from the fifth note (G) of the C major scale builds a G7 chord.   This chord has the note B (Ti) as the third of the chord.   It also has the note F (Fa) as the seventh of the chord.   As you have already seen, Fa resolves to Mi and Ti resolves to Do.   This natural resolution to Do and Mi from the third and the seventh of the V7 happens only on the chord built from the fifth degree of the scale.   Consequently, the V7 is known as the dominant chord of the key.

G7 = V7 (Dominant)

root	3rd	5th	7th
sol	ti	re	fa

G7 resolves to C = I (Tonic)

Do Mi

Ti — Active half step

FA — Active half step

8. As you can now see, chords are derived from scales. Some of the tones of the scale are active and others are resting, as illustrated in the diagram in paragraph five. The tones that create the chord then, determine the active or resting nature of the chord itself. For instance, a dominant chord is an active chord because three of the four notes that create a G7, the V7 dominant chord in the key of C major, are active tones. Only the root G is considered a resting tone. The Cmaj7 or Imaj7 in the key of Cmajor would be considered resting in nature because three of the four notes are resting tones. Only the maj7th B is active.

9. I should mention at this time that this is a simple view to a complex issue. Dominant chords can be used in many places besides the fifth degree of the major scale. For instance, dominant chords can occur in minor keys on the IV to create a IV7(#11), and the bII to create a dominant chromatic approach chord sometimes called a tri-tone or bV of V substitute for the V7 of a major key . You should make it your business to do further studies in this area. I am however, going to give you a quick look at how chords are derived in both major and minor tonalities in part III of this text.

10. The main goal in part I of this text has been to illustrate that the understanding of tonality begins with the pattern of intervals

and character of the notes that create any or all major scales. There is more to a good solo than just playing a bunch of notes till it sounds right. If you can understand the structure of the composition you will be able to attack from a strong position.

Part II
A Linear and Non Linear Approach to 5, 6, and 7 Note Scales

11. I use the term <u>Linear</u> improvisation to indicate a traditional melody based solo that moves in a scale like fashion. Soloists such as Grover Washington Jr., George Benson are good examples of linear soloists.

12. The term <u>non-linear</u> describes improvisation that utilizes traditional scales but, not in the normal sequence of mostly alphabetical order. In fact, the majority of intervals are based on 4ths, and 5ths. A good example of a non-linear composition is "Freedom Jazz Dance" by Eddie Harris. This Composition can be found in the "Real Book".

13. Five adjacent notes and 7 adjacent notes on the circle of 5ths create a pentatonic and a Major scale, as illustrated in the following diagram. As you can see. The normal Do-Re-Mi-Fa-Sol-La-Ti-Do, alphabetical order, structure is displaced when the notes of a scale are placed on the circle because, the circle arranges notes a fourth or a fifth apart. However, the original notes of the scale are not altered in any way. Clockwise or counterclockwise motion on the circle would therefore, be a non-linear approach to a traditional scale.

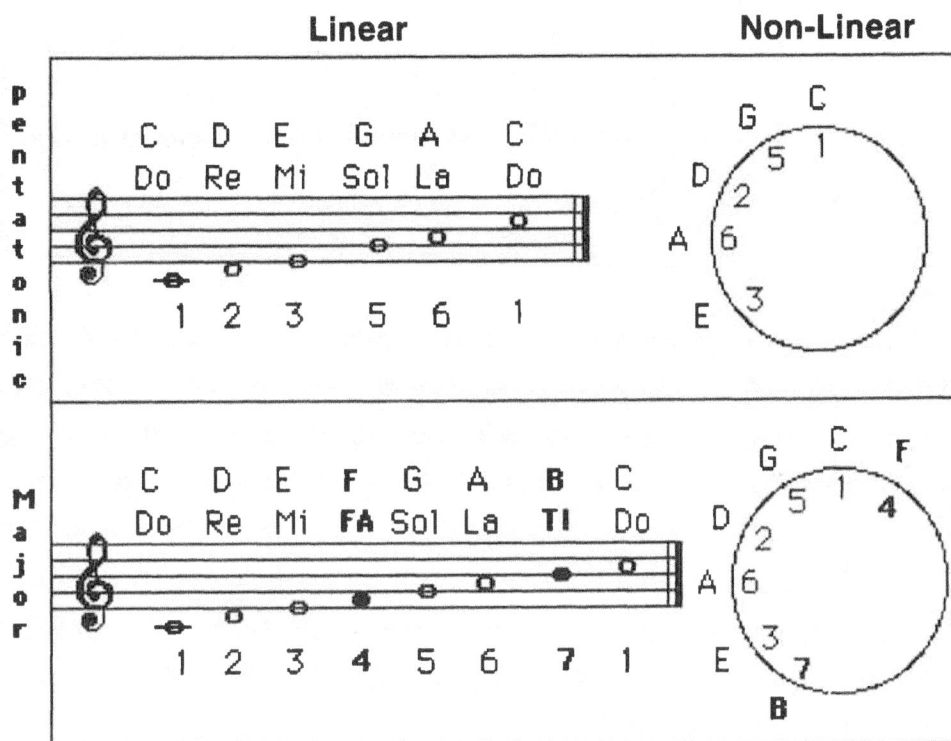

	Linear	Non-Linear

Pentatonic

C D E G A C
Do Re Mi Sol La Do

1 2 3 5 6 1

Major

C D E F G A B C
Do Re Mi FA Sol La TI Do

1 2 3 4 5 6 7 1

14.   You should also notice that the notes added to the five note pentatonic scale to create the completed seven note major scale are Ti (B) and F (Mi). As you already know, these are the active half steps that define the tonality of the Scale. Consequently, we have to assume that the five note pentatonic scale is not definitive of the tonality because it lacks the active half steps that create the dominant chord. As a matter of fact, any five adjacent pitches on the circle create a pentatonic scale. Therefore, hidden inside of the C major Scale is an F pentatonic, and a G pentatonic scale. It is possible to find five adjacent letters from each of the the notes C, F, and G. These three pentatonic scales found inside the C major scale are illustrated in the following diagram. The five dark bold letters of each circle represent the notes of each pentatonic scale.

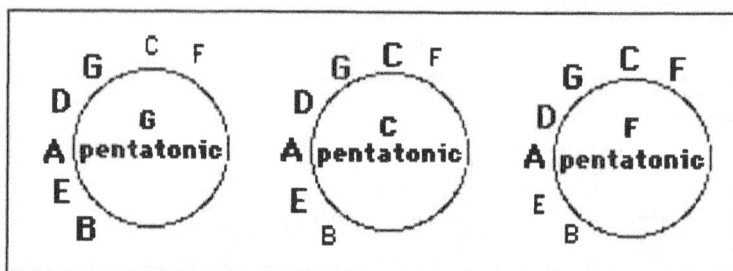

15.   It would be possible to play each of these three five note pentatonic scales as a source of melody notes when improvising in the key of C major. Each five note pentatonic scale, either G, C, or F, could be played in a linear fashion or a non-linear fashion to create the effect you desire your improvisation to have. You also have the option to combine all three pentatonic scales or, use the entire seven note major major scale in a linear or non-linear fashion. As you can see, you have a lot of options and choices to make when creating your improvisation.

16.   Before we leave the five note and seven note scales and talk about a six note scale. We need to look at an additional five note scale. The five note minor pentatonic scale is derived by playing the same notes as the original major pentatonic from the sixth note The following diagram illustrates this relationship. Therefore, any time you use a C major pentatonic scale you may also use the A minor pentatonic scale as well. Notice that the non-linear form of a minor pentatonic is the same as the non-linear form of a major pentatonic scale by comparing the following non-linear diagram to the non-linear diagram in paragraph thirteen.

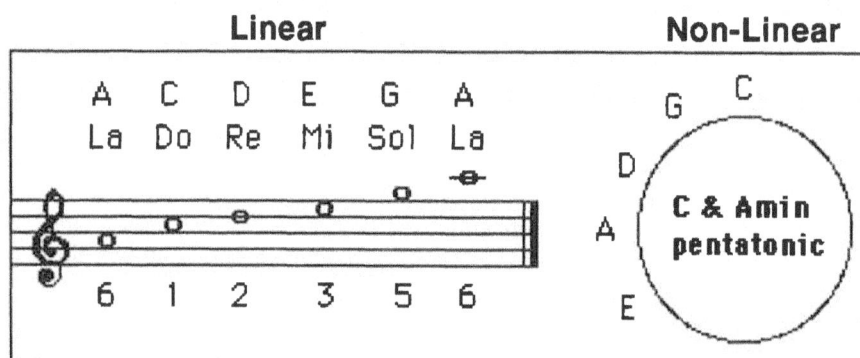

17. By adding the raised second degree to the five note A minor pentatonic scale you get a six note A blues scale. This scale can be used anytime the minor pentatonic scale is used. The added note results in an added color, or blue note, to your improvisation.

18. The following diagram is exactly the same as the diagram in paragraph sixteen. However, the raised second degree has been added. Notice that the raised second is always going to be on the other side of the circle at the point of a triangle. The starting note, or root, of the minor pentatonic scale will always be the middle note at the base of the triangle.

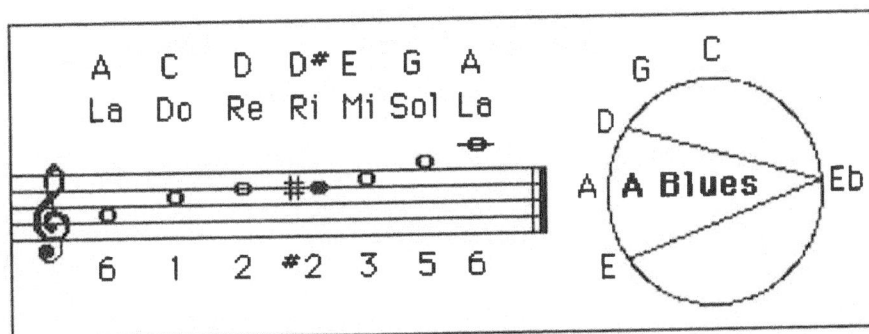

19. There is an additional seven note major and five note pentatonic that we must also consider as a possibility when improvising. The lydian scale is a scale used to play over the I chord in a major key. The lydian scale raises the fourth degree by one half step. This eliminates the clash between the half step mi to fa (E to F in the key of C major). Therefore, a C lydian scale would contain the notes C D E F# G A B C. Consequently, this can also be thought of as the key of G starting on C.

20. The following diagram illustrates the linear and non-linear version of a seven note C lydian scale. You should notice that the non-linear version of the seven note C lydian scale and the seven note G major scale would be the same. This also allows the possibility of playing five notes clockwise from F# resulting in a five note D pentatonic scale.

G Major-C Lydian-D Pentatonic

21. The following diagram illustrates all the possible five, six, and seven note scales in the tonality of C major and A Minor.

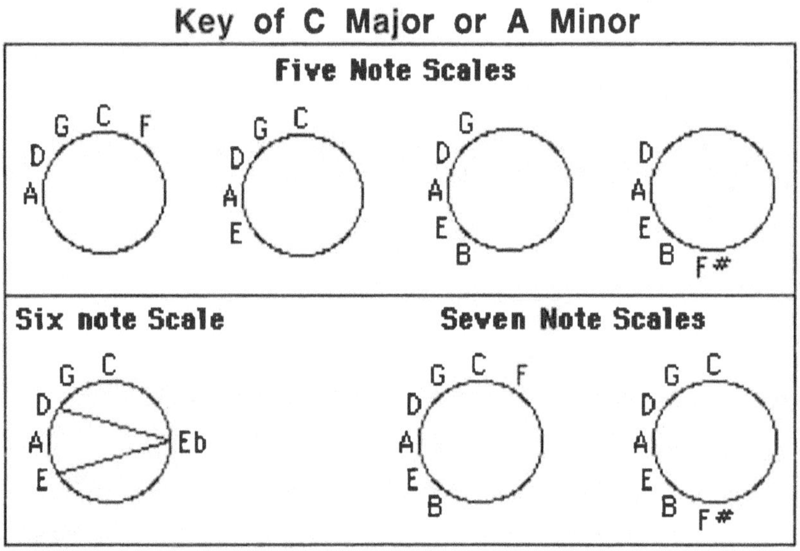

Key of C Major or A Minor

22. The song "Autumn Leaves" provides a good song to apply this concept of linear and non-linear improvisation. As you already know, the key signature has one sharp which is the key of G major or E minor. Therefore we could apply the seven note G major scale, seven note D major scale, five note G pentatonic, C pentatonic, D pentatonic, A pentatonic, E minor pentatonic, or E Blues scales as a source of melody notes to create an improvised melody. Fill in all the notes of the following diagrams using the previous diagram as an example. Use the diagram in the Key of G Major or E minor to practice this concept on "Autumn Leaves".

9

Non-Linear Exercise in all Tonalities

Key of C Major or A Minor
Five Note Scales

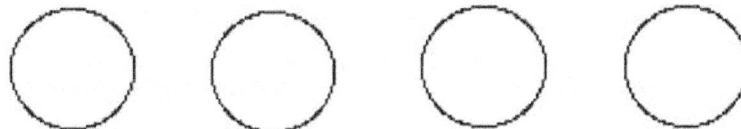

○ ○ ○ ○

Six note Scale   **Seven Note Scales**

○   ○ ○

Key of F Major or D Minor
Five Note Scales

○ ○ ○ ○

Six note Scale   **Seven Note Scales**

○   ○ ○

Key of Bb Major or G Minor
Five Note Scales

○ ○ ○ ○

Six note Scale   **Seven Note Scales**

○   ○ ○

Key of Eb Major or C Minor
Five Note Scales

○ ○ ○ ○

Six note Scale   **Seven Note Scales**

○   ○ ○

11

Key of Ab Major or F Minor
Five Note Scales

Six note Scale   Seven Note Scales

Key of Db Major or Bb minor
Five Note Scales

Six note Scale   Seven Note Scales

Key of Gb Major or Eb Minor
Five Note Scales

○ ○ ○ ○

Six note Scale   **Seven Note Scales**

○   ○ ○

Key of B Major or G# Minor
Five Note Scales

○ ○ ○ ○

Six note Scale   **Seven Note Scales**

○   ○ ○

Key of E Major or C# Minor
Five Note Scales

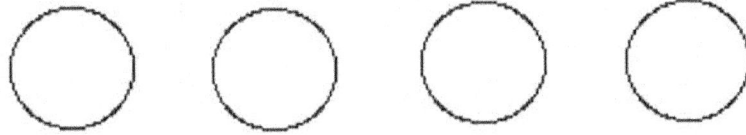

Six note Scale   Seven Note Scales

Key of A major or F# Minor
Five Note Scales

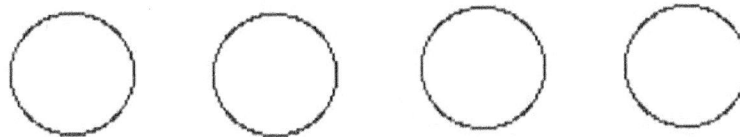

Six note Scale   Seven Note Scales

14

Key of D Major or B Minor
Five Note Scales

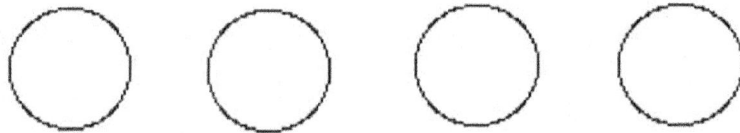

Six note Scale   Seven Note Scales

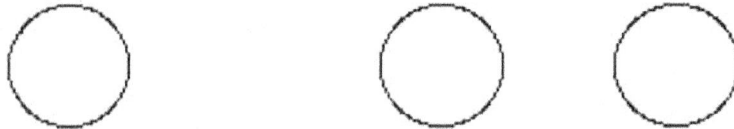

Key of G Major or E Minor
Five Note Scales

Six note Scale   Seven Note Scales

23. The following diagram illustrates four note chords built from each note of a C major scale. Therefore, each chord has a function or role that it plays in the tonality. The chord built from the first note of the scale is a Cmaj7 and is considered the Imaj7. Maj7 chords also occur on the fourth degree of the major scale. The chord built from the fifth degree is a V7 known as the dominant chord as you have already seen in paragraph seven. The chords built from the II, III, and VI are min7 chords and finally the chord built from the seventh degree is min7(b5).

Key of C Major Diatonic Four Note Chords

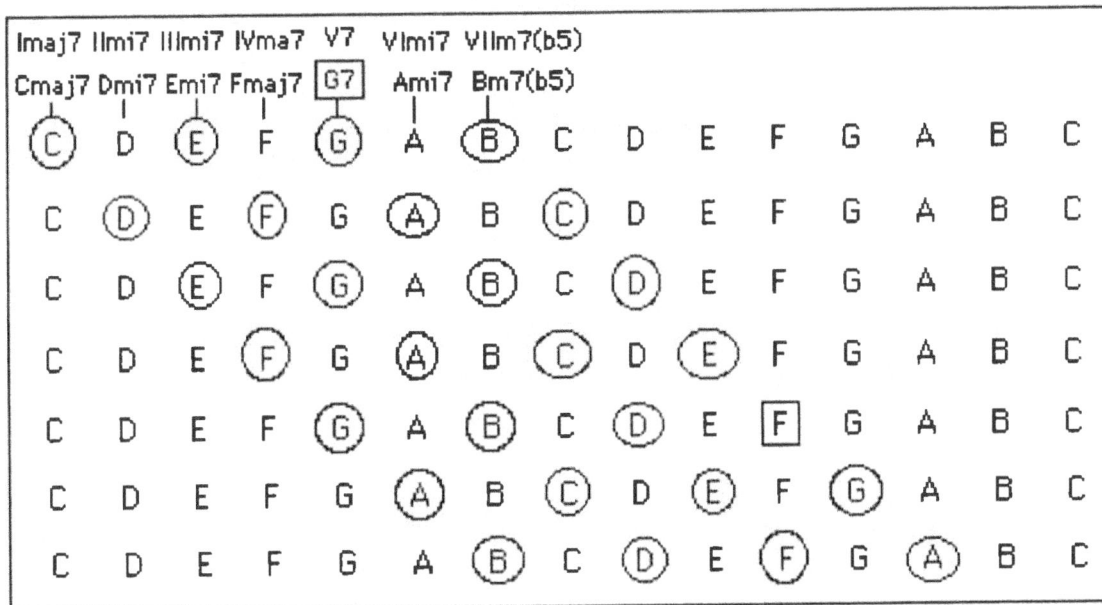

Imaj7	IImi7	IIImi7	IVma7	V7	VImi7	VIIm7(b5)
Cmaj7	Dmi7	Emi7	Fmaj7	G7	Ami7	Bm7(b5)

```
(C)  D  (E)  F  (G)  A  (B)  C   D   E   F   G   A   B   C
 C  (D)  E  (F)  G  (A)  B  (C)  D   E   F   G   A   B   C
 C   D  (E)  F  (G)  A  (B)  C  (D)  E   F   G   A   B   C
 C   D   E  (F)  G  (A)  B  (C)  D  (E)  F   G   A   B   C
 C   D   E   F  (G)  A  (B)  C  (D)  E  [F]  G   A   B   C
 C   D   E   F   G  (A)  B  (C)  D  (E)  F  (G)  A   B   C
 C   D   E   F   G   A  (B)  C  (D)  E  (F)  G  (A)  B   C
```

Diatonic Chord Pattern for Major Tonalities:

I & IV   = maj7

II, III, & VI   = min7

VII   = min7(b5)

16

24. Any five, six, or seven note scale for the key of C major or A minor, played in a linear or non-linear fashion, would provide a source of melody notes for an improvisation over chords from the diagram in paragraph twenty three. The chords could be placed in various orders but, the tonality would remain the same.

25. One each of the five and seven note scales lend themselves to the function of the Imaj7 or I lydian scale as presented in paragraphs nineteen and twenty. All of the other five, six, and seven note scales can be played over the IImi7, IIImi7, IVmaj7, V7, VImi7, and VIImi7(b5) of the tonality.

Key of C Major

Five Note Scales

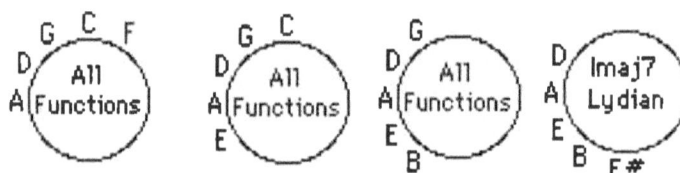

Six note Scale

Seven Note Scales

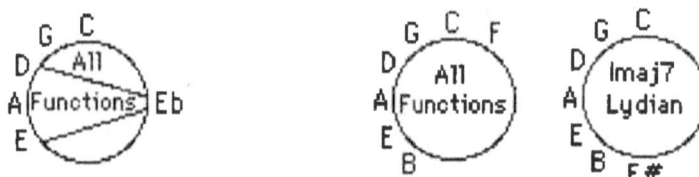

26. The previous diagram illustrates that all maj7th chords that function as a I of the major tonality should be treated as a lydian scale rather than a major scale.

27. Minor scales are derived by altering a major scale. The following diagram illustrates the appropriate alterations.

Natural Minor: 1   2   b3 4   5   b6 b7 1
                  C   D   Eb F   G   Ab Bb C

Melodic Minor:	1	2	b3	4	5	6	7	1
	C	D	Eb	F	G	A	B	C

Harmonic Minor:	1	2	b3	4	5	b6	7	1
	C	D	Eb	F	G	Ab	B	C

28.   As you can guess, this would also change the spelling of the chords.   Some of the original seven chords diatonic to the major scale would now have altered notes.   These notes would then need to be indicated in a parenthesis placed next to the original chord symbol.   For example, Dmi7 was the IImin7 in the key of C major. The diagram in paragraph twenty three shows that Dmi7 is spelled D-F-A-C.   However, in both the C natural minor and C harmonic minor in paragraph twenty seven, the A is flatted.   Therefore, the Dmi7 in a major key becomes Dmi7(b5) in a minor key.   The G7 or dominant chord in a major key is spelled G-B-D-F.   If you continued up to the ninth it would become G9 or G-B-D-F-A.   In the harmonic minor scale the A, again, would be flatted and the chord would become G7(b9). The following diagram illustrates what happens to the chords of a major scale when they are altered to become the chords of a minor scale.   Notice that there is a difference between parallel and relative minor.

1. Unaltered Major

3. Relative Minor
(of unaltered Major)

IMaj7	IImi7	IIImi7	IVmaj7	V9	VImi7	VIImi7(b5)
Cmaj7	Dmi7	Emi7	Fmaj7	G9	Ami7	Bmi7(b5)
C6			F6			* E7(b9)

2. Altered Major
(Parallel Minor)

Imin	IImi7(b5)		V7(b9)
Cmin	Dmi7(b5)		G7(b9)
Cmi6			
Cmi7			
CmiMaj7			
Cmi(add9)			

29.   The following diagram further illustrates the II-V-I relationships found within the unaltered major, parallel minor, and the relative minor.   Notice that the Imin and the IImi7(b5) in the relative minor are also the VImi7 and the VIImi7(b5) in the previous diagram.   To obtain the V7(b9) of the relative minor the Emin7 had the third (G) raised one half step (G#) to become E7.   This E7 functions as a V in the relative minor therefore, the ninth would be F which is a flatted ninth degree above the root E.   The only note that does not belong to the major scale is the G#.   Consequently, you could think of relative minor as raising a pitch of the major scale as opposed to parallel minor which you have already seen lowers pitches of the major scale.

19

1. Unaltered Major

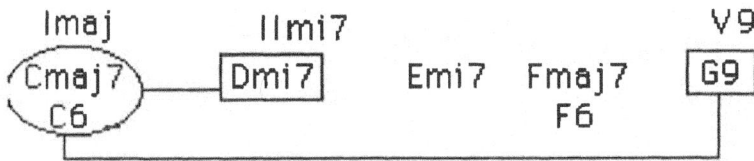

Imaj   IImi7   V9

(Cmaj7 / C6) — [Dmi7]   Emi7   Fmaj7 / F6   [G9]

3. Relative Minor

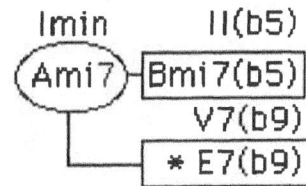

Imin   II(b5)

(Ami7) — [Bmi7(b5)]

V7(b9)

[* E7(b9)]

2. Parallel Minor (altered Major)

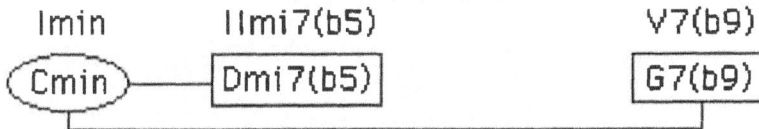

Imin   IImi7(b5)   V7(b9)

(Cmin) — [Dmi7(b5)]   [G7(b9)]

30.. The following diagrams illustrates the five, six, and seven note scales to be used over C major & A relative minor. This diagram could also be used for parallel minor. For example, A minor would be the parallel minor of A major.

Unaltered C Major and A Minor (relative minor)

Five Note Scales

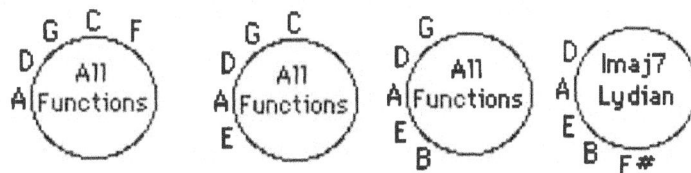

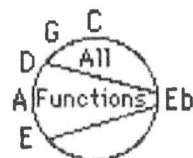

Circle 1: G, C, F / D, A — All Functions

Circle 2: G, C / D, A, E — All Functions

Circle 3: G / D, A, E, B — All Functions

Circle 4: D, A, E, B, F# — Imaj7 Lydian

Six note Scale	Seven Note Scales

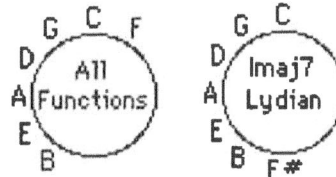

Six note Scale circle: G, C / D, A, E + Eb — All Functions

Seven Note Scales circle 1: G, C, F / D, A, E, B — All Functions

Seven Note Scales circle 2: G, C / D, A, E, B, F# — Imaj7 Lydian

31. If you wanted to play the parallel minor of C major you would have to use Eb major and C minor as illustrated in the following diagram.

Five Note Scales

O C f Bb   G CF   CF Bb D
      Eb   OG   A G C F
      Ab   o:b

Six note Scale   **Seven Note Scales**

A7'fb   O C F Bb   DOG CF Bb
                                        Eb   A   Eb
\ J j _) Eb   Ab
      Gb

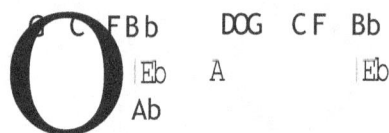

32.   The tune "Wave" by Jobim, which can be found in the "Real Book", is a great example of this concept of unaltered major and parallel minor.   The first chord of the <u>A section,</u> after the introduction, is Dmaj7 and the melody in the first eight measures is based on the D major scale with the exception of two notes.   There is a Bb on the second half of beat one in measure two and an Ab on the second half of beat two in measure eight.   The next four bars are based on the D blues scale and the chords resolve to Dmin7.   Therefore, the song goes from D major (unaltered major) to D minor (parallel minor). The following diagrams illustrate this change.

First Eight Measures of the **A Section** for "Wave" by Jobim
Key of D Major or B Minor

Five Note Scales

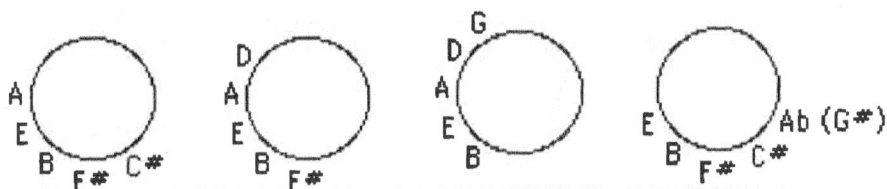

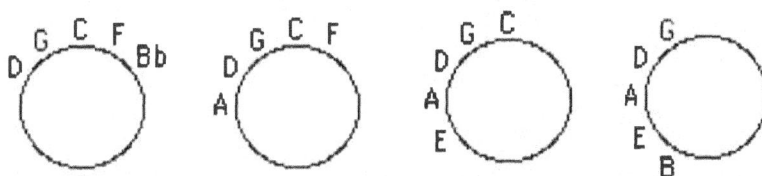

Six note Scale

Seven Note Scales

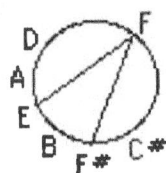

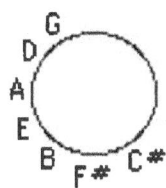

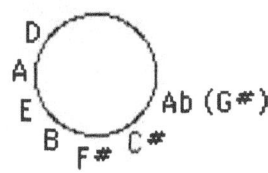

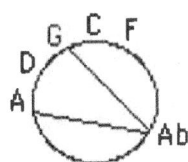

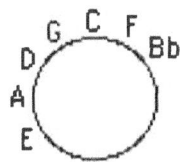

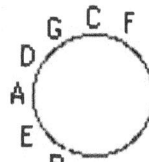

Last Four Measures of the **A Section** for "Wave" by Jobim
Key of F Major or D Minor

Five Note Scales

Six note Scale

Seven Note Scales

33. The B section or "Bridge" of "Wave" is eight measures in length. The first four measures are in the key of F major, and the last four measures are in the key of Eb major. The following diagrams illustrate the scales to use over the bridge.

22

First Four Measures of the <u>B Section</u> for "Wave" by Jobim
Key of F Major or D Minor

Five Note Scales

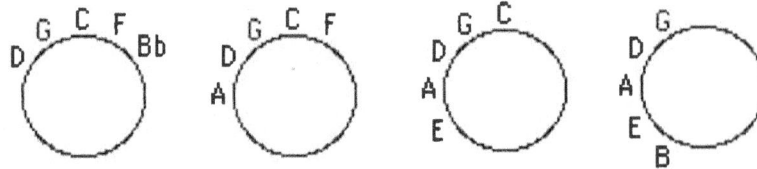

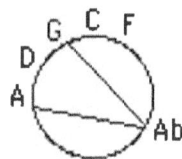

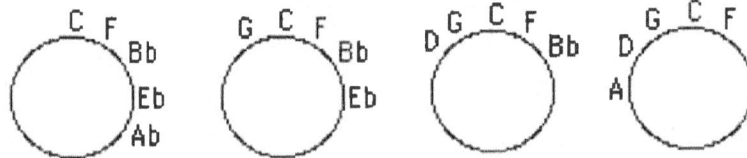

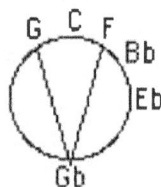

Six note Scale   **Seven Note Scales**

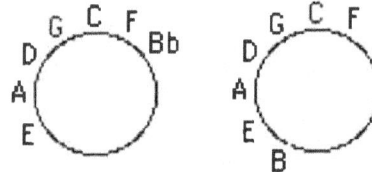

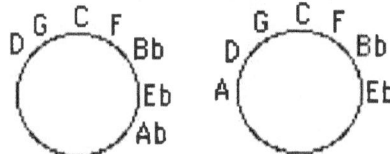

Last Four Measures of the <u>B Section</u> for "Wave" by Jobim
Key of Eb Major or C Minor

Five Note Scales

Six note Scale   **Seven Note Scales**

34.   One particular kind of chord function that can be used in connection with a major, parallel minor, or relative minor tonality without moving to an additional five, six, or seven note scale is the dominant chromatic approach chord. Some of you may already know this as the "Tri-Tone Substitute" or the "bV of V Substitute". The following diagram illustrates that a dominant chromatic approach chord moves to a diatonic chord from above moving downward by half step. In this situation you can alter the 11th degree by raising

23

it one half step. You should notice that the raised 11th of all dominant chromatic approach chords combined, creates a G major or C Lydian scale. Therefore, even though most of the roots of the dominant chromatic approach chords are chromatic to the tonality, the alteration of the chord will always remain diatonic to the tonality. This use of the dominant chromatic approach chord can be found in the tune "Autumn Leaves" in measures twenty seven and twenty eight. The progression is Emi7 to Eb7 to Dmi7 to Db7 to Cmaj7. The Eb7 moves down to Dmi7 and the Db7 moves down to Cmaj7. The raised 11th of Eb7 is A and the raised 11th of Db is G. These notes are obviously diatonic to the tonality of E minor relative to G major.

Dominant Chromatic Approach Chords

Db7 ↘Cmaj7 C6 Cmin	Eb7 ↘Dmi7 Dmin7(b5)	F7 ↘Emi7	Gb7 ↘Fmaj7 F6	Ab7 ↘G9 G7(b9)	Bb7 ↘Ami7	C7 ↘Bmi7(b5)

#11 of	Db7	Eb7	F7	Gb7	Ab7	Bb7	C7
is	G	A	B	C	D	E	F#

G Major or C Lydian Scale

35. Another common tool that can be used in connection with a major, parallel minor, or relative minor tonality without moving to an additional five, six, or seven note scale is the additional II-V leading to a diatonic function of the major scale. This is illustrated in the following diagram. Notice that there is an additional altered II-V preceding the Dmin7 and the Emin7 as well as an unaltered II-V preceding the Fmaj7. These additional II-V's give the listener the impression that the song momentarily went to either Dmin, Emin, or F maj however, in reality everything still remains in the key of C major or A minor. Consequently, any five, six, or seven note scale that applies to the key of C major or A minor would still be applied.

24

Additional II-V'S Preceding Diatonic II, III, & IV Chords

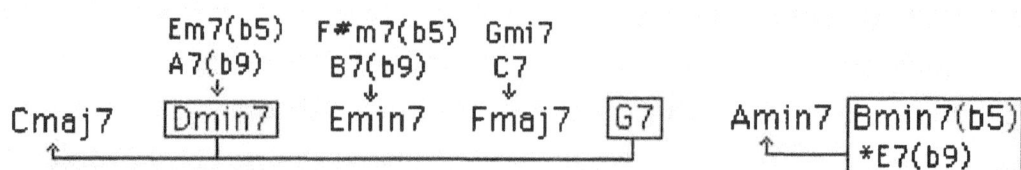

```
        Em7(b5)   F#m7(b5)  Gmi7
        A7(b9)    B7(b9)    C7
          ↓         ↓        ↓
Cmaj7   |Dmin7|  Emin7   Fmaj7  |G7|      Amin7  |Bmin7(b5)|
  ↑_____|_____|          ↑_____|*E7(b9)  |
```

36. Occasionally, a V7 will precede another unaltered V7 in a major key, or an altered V7(b9) in a minor key. The following diagram illustrates this. In the key of C major the G7, or V7 of the key of C, could be preceded by both Ami7 and D7. This also means that the E7(b9), the V7(b9) of Amin, could be preceded by both F#mi7(b5) and B7(b9). I should mention however, that often just the additional V is used therefore, omitting the additional II.

Additional II-V Preceding the V7 in Major & V7(b9) in Relative Minor

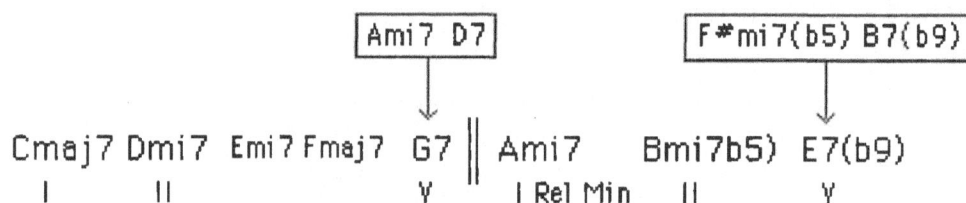

```
                        |Ami7 D7|              |F#mi7(b5) B7(b9)|
                           ↓                          ↓
Cmaj7 Dmi7 Emi7 Fmaj7   G7  ‖ Ami7      Bmi7b5)    E7(b9)
  I        II            V     I Rel Min   II         V
```

37. The tune "Lucky Southern", which can be found in the real book, has examples of many of these tools. A dominant chromatic approach chord, Bb7 approaching A7 by half step, is used in measures six, fourteen, and thirty. The E7 in measures three and eleven is not diatonic to the key of D major however, it is the V7 of A7 as in the diagram found in paragraph thirty six. This E7 is an additional V preceding the V7 without the II which would have been Bmi7. Finally, in measures twenty three and twenty four, the Amin7 to D7 is an additional II-V preceding the diatonic IVmaj7 chord which is Gmaj7.

38. The following diagram would be the the five, six, and seven note scales which can be used as a source of melody notes for an improvisation over the entire progression for "Lucky Southern".

Key of D Major or B Minor

Five Note Scales

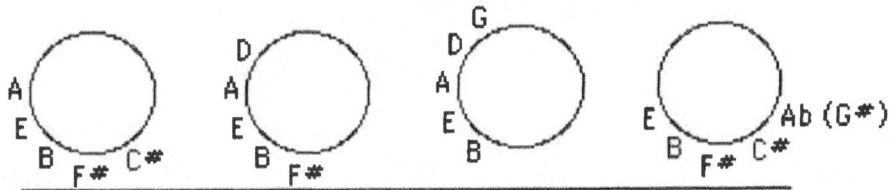

Six note Scale   Seven Note Scales

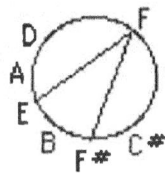

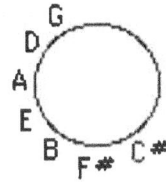

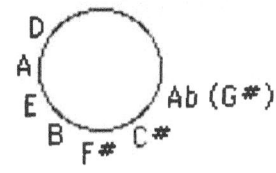

39. In conclusion to Part III of this text, the following diagram illustrates how each diatonic chord can ultimately be approached with its own II-V. Each diatonic chord can also be approached from above by half step, and below by half step.

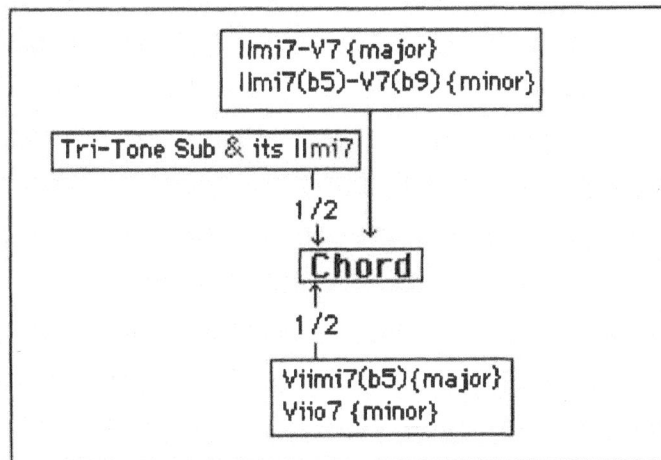

40. The following diagram entitled "Tonality of C Major and A Minor" is an example of the previous diagram applied to the diatonic chords of a C major and A natural minor scale. Consequently, any of these functions that occur while the tonality of the song remains in the key of C major or A minor will not require any additional momentary scales. The song "Black Orpheus" by Louis Bonfi would be a good song for study to solidify this concept.

26

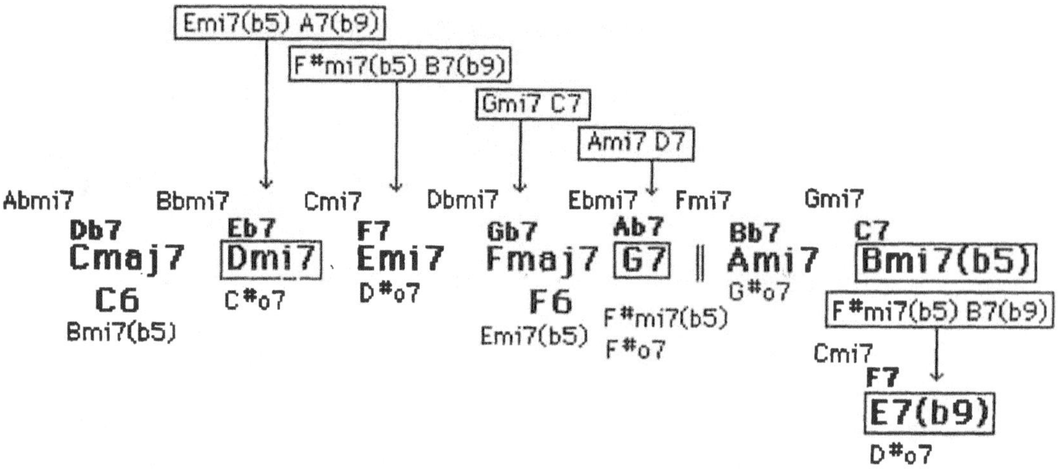

Part IV
12 Note Scales

41.   Up to this point we have discussed five, six, and seven note scales.   However, the chromatic scale is a very important scale as it contains all the notes that build all tonalities.   Historically, the use of chromaticism within a diatonic setting, or tonality, began to appear in the "Romantic" or 19th century period of music.   At that time it was simply called the rising semi-tone.   The rising semi-tone is demonstrated in the following diagram.   Each note of the C major scale is preceded by a rising semi-tone.   This is now known as a lower neighbor tone which can be defined as a note one half step below a scale tone, or chord tone, approaching from below.   Some people also call this an approach tone.   As you can see, the seven note major scale plus the five chromatic pitches created by adding the lower neighbor, or approach tones, creates a twelve note scale.

♩. = Scale Tone
LN = LOWER NEIGHBOR TONE (APPROACH TONE)

27

42. Traditional linear improvisations require that diatonic pitches be played on the downbeats of the strong beats one and three in a 4/4 time signature or beat one in a 3/4 time signature. This means that the chromatic pitches can be played on the + or upbeat of any beat as well as any downbeat that is not considered a strong beat. In a 4/4 time signature the weak beats would be beats two and four, and beats two and three in a 3/4 time signature. Consequently, the tonality of the composition is not disturbed because the rhythmic strong points of the song remain diatonic.

43. The following diagram illustrates how the lower neighbor tones are simply the remaining pitches of the circle after the seven note major scale is accounted for. You must also remember that the notes of the C major scale are the same for the modes relative to the key of C such as, D Dorian and G mixolydian.

12 Note Scale C Major/D Dorian/G Mixolydian Combined
With Lower Neighbors

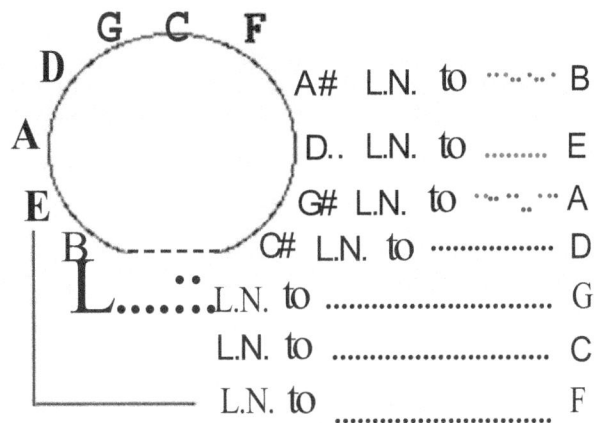

A# L.N. to .... B

D.. L.N. to .... E

G# L.N. to .... A

C# L.N. to .... D

L.N. to .... G

L.N. to C

L.N. to .... F

44. Non-linear soloing throws the tonality out of the window to a certain degree. Only beat one of a two bar or four bar phrase need to remain diatonic. As you can already guess, this approach will have a tendency to be more outside. A floating effect can be felt because many of the lower neighbor tones will fall on downbeats. However, if the end of the phrase leads into a diatonic pitch on the downbeat of beat one in the new phrase this floating effect will be resolved.

45. The tune "Impressions by" John Coltrane, which can be found in the Real Book, is a very good tune to practice a linear and non-linear approach to lower neighbor tones. There are only two chords, Dmi7 and Ebmi7. The Dmi7 indicates that the scale would be D Dorian relative to the key of C major. Therefore, the seven note C major scale and its lower neighbor tones would be used as a source of notes from which to create an improvisation. When the the tune goes up one half step to Ebmi7 the key also moves up to the seven note Db major scale and its lower neighbor tones.

46. Another composition that I mentioned in paragraph twelve, "Freedom Jazz Dance" by Eddie Harris, is based on one chord and therefore, is a good song to practice using lower neighbor tones. The only chord for this composition is Bb7 which represents a Bb mixolydian scale relative to the key of Eb major. Consequently, the seven note Eb major scale and its lower neighbor tones would be used as a source of melody notes for an improvisation.

47. I mention the two tunes "Impressions" and "Freedom Jazz Dance" because they stay in one key long enough to practice a new concept. However, this idea of using lower neighbor tones can be applied to any song once you have it in your fingers and ears. You will find that once you begin to be familiar with playing the lower neighbor tones they will simply become part of your normal way of playing.

Part V
Symmetric Scales & Non-Linear Improvisation

48. The word symmetric is an adjective to describe something as having regularity and balance. Music has many examples of symmetry. Each note of an augmented triad and dim 7th chord is an equal distance apart. Consequently, any note of the original chord can serve as a root. For example, a C augmented triad contains the notes C, E, and G#(Ab). The E, and Ab augmented triads consist of the same three notes as the C augmented triad. This is symmetry.

49. The symmetrical augmented triad is derived from the whole tone scale which is a series of (whole step) equal distances. Therefore, the whole tone scale is a six note symmetric scale. Consequently, since there are only twelve pitches there are only two whole tone scales.

50. The following diagram illustrates these two whole tone scales and all the four note altered dominant chords derived from them. The notes on the staff are both scales combined into a twelve note scale. The circled notes are from the C# whole tone scale and connect to each note of the C whole tone scale by a fifth or fourth. Notice also that this is simply the circle moving counterclockwise or, a seven note C major scale with its lower neighbor tones.

Symmetric Whole Tone Scales

	C+7	D+7	E+7	F#+7	Ab+7	Bb+7	C+7
C Whole Tone	C	D	E	F#	G#	Bb	C
C# Whole Tone	C#	D#	F	G	A	B	C#
	C#+7	D#+7	F+7	G+7	A+7	B+7	C#+7

51. Another symmetric scale is the eight note diminished scale. This scale gets its name from the diminished 7th chord. The Co7 chord is derived from the eight note C diminished scale. This eight note scale is regular intervals of a whole then a half step. For example C up a whole step to D then up a half step to Eb, then continuing by whole and then half steps. The eight note C diminished scale would consist of the notes **C**-D-**D#**-F-**F#**-G#-**A**-B-C. Every other letter of this scale creates a Co7 chord. As I mentioned in paragraph forty six, any note of a dim 7th chord can serve as a root. Consequently, Co7 is also D#o7, F#o7, and Ao7. This happens because the distance from each note in the dim 7th chord is three

half steps apart which divides the twelve chromatic pitches into four equal divisions. This is also why there are only three diminished scales. Twelve divided by four is three. The following diagram illustrates these three Diminished scales and each of the dim 7th and altered dominant chords related to each scale. You should also know that the dim 7th chord is the same as a dominant flat nine minus the root. For example, an Ab7(b9) chord is spelled from the root up, **Ab-C-Eb-Gb-Bbb** and Co7 is spelled **C-Eb-Gb-Bbb.** As you can see, these are the same notes without the Ab, which is the root of the Ab7(b9).

Eight Note Diminished Scales and the Chords Derived From Them

C Diminished 8-Note			
Ab7(b9)	B7(b9)	D7(b9)	F7(b9)
Co7	D#o7	F#o7	Ao7

C#Diminished 8-Note			
A7(b9)	C7(b9)	Eb7(b9)	Gb7(b9)
C#o7	Eo7	Go7	Bbo7

D Diminished 8-Note			
Bb7(b9)	Db7(b9)	E7(b9)	G7(b9)
Do7	Fo7	G#o7	Bo7

52. By connecting each note of a diminished scale with the interval of a fourth or a fifth, as illustrated in the following diagram, the twelve note chromatic scale is achieved. Also illustrated in this diagram are the four altered dominant chords created by the C diminished eight note scale. Remember, there are only three diminished scales. Therefore, each eight note diminished scale contains four dominant chords. Three scales times four dominant chords equals twelve keys.

Creating a Twelve Note Scale from an Eight Note Diminished Scale

C Diminished 8-Note Scale

3	+11	5	13	b7	1	b9	+9	3	= Ab7(b9)
b9	+9	3	+11	5	13	b7	1	b9	= B7(b9)
b7	1	b9	+9	3	+11	5	13	b7	= D7(b9)
5	13	b7	1	b9	+9	3	+11	5	= F7(b9)
C	D	Eb	F	Gb	Ab	A	B	C	

whole half whole half whole half whole half

C   D   Eb   F   Gb   Ab   A   B   C

‡The circled notes connect each whole step by a fifth or a fourth.
They also add the missing four notes to complete a 12 note scale.

53. The four circled notes in the previous diagram are placed only between the notes that are a whole step away. The whole step movement is made stronger by the addition of the notes that connect by fifths and fourths. The notes that are one half step away do not need this additional connection because they are already smoothly connected. As you already know, the half step is the strongest possible movement.

54. Another much used symmetric scale is the eight note dominant scale. It is created by playing regular intervals of half-whole-half-whole...etc. In reality, it is the exact same scale as the eight note diminished. The only difference is that the eight note dominant scale is played from the root of the V7(b9) and the eight note diminished scale is played from the 5th degree of the V7(b9). For example, the eight note dominant scale for G7(b9) would be the G eight note dominant (from the root) and the eight note diminished scale would be built from the 5th or D eight note diminished scale.

32

Comparison of 8 Note Dominant & Diminished Scales for G7(b9)

G Eight Note Dominant Scale Built From the Root
G-Ab-Bb-8-C#-D-E-F-G

D Eight Note Diminished Scale Built From the 5th
D-E-F-G-Ab-Bb-B-C#-D

55. As you can see, both the G eight note dominant and the D eight note diminished scales contain the same notes. Consequently, the pattern you learn for the eight note diminished scale in paragraph fifty will also apply to an eight note dominant scale.

56. This completes the "Simplified Guide to Jazz Improvisation; Linear and Non-Linear". I know that if you have gone through this guide and practiced each new concept that your improvisations have become more interesting and hopefully more musical as well. If you would like to discuss any part of this text you may reach me at the following numbers:

NEW MEXICO   1+505-238-2966

Raven Ridge Drive NE, Albuq., NM 87113

Biographical Information: Terry Janow, a recipient of a Jazz Fellowship from the National Endowment for the Arts in 1979 has performed in the 505th and 761st Air Force Bands (1970-74) as well as television and movie scores. Terry has performed in concert with such notables as Anita O'Day, the "Temptations", Freddie Fender and many more. Terry was the Director of the General Musicianship Program at the "Grove School of Music" from 1983 until 1991 when he founded T.J. Music Consultation and T.J. Music Consultation Publications. Terry is currently active as a session player/composer, author/educator and can be found lecturing at clinics & seminars throughout the United States as well as maintaining a private teaching practice.

www.ingramcontent.com/pod-product-compliance
Lightning Source LLC
LaVergne TN
LVHW082323080426

835508LV00042B/1527